Albatros Fighters
in action

by John F. Connors

illustrated by Don Greer

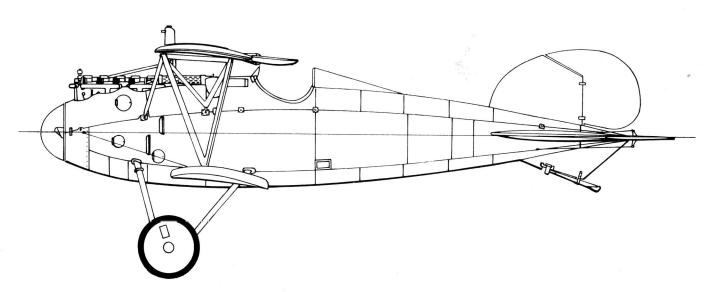

squadron/signal publications

(Cover) When handled with skill and courage, the Albatros was able to master any aircraft the RAF could throw at it. During the hard winter of 1917-18, Albatros D.Va of Jasta 12 maneuvers for favorable position on a pair of S.E.5as.

If you have any photographs of the aircraft, armor, soldiers or ships of any nation, particularly wartime snapshots, why not share them with us and help make Squadron/Signal's books all the more interesting and complete in the future. Any photograph sent to us will be copied and the original returned. The donor will be fully credited for any photos used. Please send them to: Squadron/Signal Publications, Inc., 1115 Crowley Dr., Carrollton, TX 75006.

ISBN 0-89747-115-6

Author's Note

It is most significant that the initial World War One subject to be covered by Squadron/Signal's **in Action** series should be the Albatros fighters. From the fall of 1916 until the end of the war, the Albatros was the mainstay of fighter units of the Imperial German Air Service. Even though out-moded by more sophisticated aircraft later in the war, the Albatros, like the Messerschmitt Bf 109 of World War Two, remained the backbone of the German fighter forces. Nearly every well-known German ace of the First World War flew an Albatros at some time in his career, if not for most of it. Having been flown by so many aces, and having seen so much combat service, Albatros fighters carried some of the most colorful and fascinating personal and unit markings ever seen on military aircraft, as the color pages of this book will attest.

Special thanks are due to John R. Carlson, whose collection provided most of the photographs for this book; also to Peter M. Grosz, the Air Force Museum and the National Air and Space Museum for additional information and guidance. Thanks also to Robert Sheldon, whose extensive private library was always at my disposal.

Finally, a word of appreciation to Dan Abbot, who was a great help in identifying color schemes.

All photos courtesy John R. Carlson collection, unless otherwise noted.

To Kim & Pat

(Opposite) A flight of Albatros D.Vas of Jasta 8 with black and white tail stripes. By this time, in late 1917, the Albatros no longer enjoyed the superiority it had a year earlier. Still, in the hands of a skilled pilot, it could master any Allied opponent.

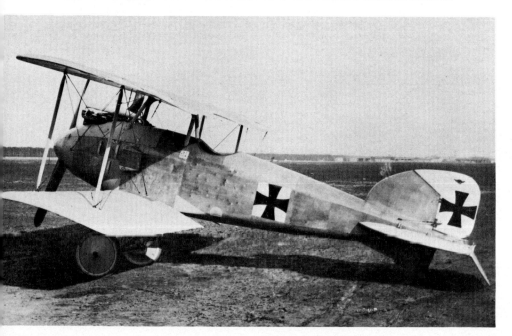

Introduction:
The Albatros D.I

The *Albatros-Flugzeugwerke* GmbH was founded at Johannistahl in 1910 by Walter Huth, a German aviation enthusiast. Huth owned a French-designed Farman biplane, so it is little surprise that early Albatros aircraft closely followed the Farman format. By the outbreak of war in 1914, however, the Albatros firm was engaged in the building of aircraft of original design. Albatros B and C Type two-seaters gained an early and excellent reputation among German aircrews for their speed, strength and reliability.

By the spring of 1916, the air superiority that the Germans had gained with the Fokker **Eindecker** was lost. Newer Allied aircraft, specifically the French Nieuport 11 and the British DeHavilland D.H.2, greatly outclassed the Fokker monoplanes. Neither of these Allied machines was equipped with a synchronized machine gun, pioneered by the Fokker, but both were superior in performance. In order to regain air supremacy, officials of the German Air Service called for the reorganization of fighter aircraft into more concentrated units and better aircraft to equip those units. In response to this latter demand, Albatros unveiled the **D.I** in April 1916.

The D.I was the brainchild of Robert Thelen and his assistant *Dipl. Ing.* Schubert. Thelen had joined Albatros in April 1912, as chief designer, and in the summer of 1914 was promoted to technical director. Schubert then became head of the design department. Thelen decided to concentrate on speed, power and armament, at the expense of maneuverability, and so designed the D.I around the most powerful and reliable power plant then available, the Mercedes D.III of 160hp, a six-cylinder inline engine. Two synchronized 7.92mm Maxim machine guns were mounted in front of the cockpit.

The wings, of typical construction for the time, were built around two main spars with plywood ribs and fabric covering. On the D.I prototype, the lower wing was of a slightly narrower chord than the upper; on production aircraft, the chord was made constant in order to ease production. The parallel interplane struts and the single trestle-type cabane structure were of streamlined steel tubing, mounted in bayonet type socket joints. The angle of stagger of the upper wing was adjustable.

The fuselage was of semi-monocoque construction, built around six spruce longerons which were supported by formers of three-ply. Around this frame was built a shell of three-ply sheets, tacked and screwed in place. This kind of construction resulted in a lightweight but extremely sturdy fuselage, which required no internal wire bracing. The vertical tail fin was also of wood and was integral with the fuselage, as was the raked underfin that supported the ash tail skid.

The lower wing panels were attached to an abutment that stretched below, but not wider than, the fuselage. Shaped aluminum fairings streamlined the wing root into the curved fuselage underbelly. A circular aluminum cowl formed the nose section of the fuselage on either side of the engine cylinder block. The hub of the laminated Axial propeller was encased in a bulbous aluminum spinner. The only feature that detracted from the clean appearance of the fuselage was the mounting of a Windhoff radiator on each fuselage side, between the wings.

The undercarriage was of the typical 'V'-type of steel tube struts, the axle sprung with elastic (bungee) cords. All control surfaces were of steel tube framing with fabric covering.

The D.I prototype showed excellent performance. Its top speed was 102mph, and it could climb to 1,000 meters (3,280ft) in just over four minutes. Although the performance of the D.I was met with much enthusiasm, it was not ordered into immediate production. Only 12 pre-production examples were ordered in June 1916, full-scale production not being approved until August. The reason for this delay is not known, but the D.I was ready for combat by September 1916.

The D.I made its combat debut at a time when German fighter aircraft were being reorganized into units known as **jagdstaffeln** (literally 'hunting echelons', abbreviated

Albatros D.I prototype, probably at Johannistahl, shows the clean, compact lines that made it the most modern fighter aircraft of its time. Features not incorporated on production D.Is include upswept 'rhino horn' exhaust outlet and unbalanced elevators. The prototype was unarmed. The only paint applied to this aircraft are national markings and Albatros company trademark on rudder. Note side-mounted Windhoff radiator.

The top view of this production D.I shows a camouflage pattern of dark green and chestnut brown. The fuselage is clear-varnished plywood. Note also early style national markings on close-cropped white squares. Struts and metal panels are light gray.

Jastas). **Jasta 1** was formed on 23 August 1916 at Bertincourt, under the command of *Hauptmann* Martin Zander. **Jasta 2** was formed four days later at Laguincourt and commanded by *Oberleutnant* (later *Hauptmann*) Oswald Boelcke. By the end of August, seven **Jastas** had been formed and, by the end of 1916, 26 had been organized.

Although second in numerical order, Boelcke's **Jasta 2** was the first to see action. The unit received its first Albatros D.Is in mid-September and, on the 17th of that month, Boelcke and five other pilots made their first patrol with the new aircraft. Near Cambrai, a flight of seven British F.E.2b pushers was encountered and, in the ensuing dogfight, five of the pushers were brought down with no loss to the Germans.

The D.I immediately made every other fighter aircraft at the front obsolete. Although less maneuverable than the Nieuport 11 or the D.H.2, the Albatros was faster, stronger and had twice the firepower with its two guns.

The D.I's service peak came in November 1916, when there were 50 examples at the front. Production of the D.I was limited, because the construction of its successor, the **D.II**, was begun even before the D.I entered combat. A total of 62 Albatros D.Is were built, including the 12 pre-production machines ordered in June.

Albatros Development

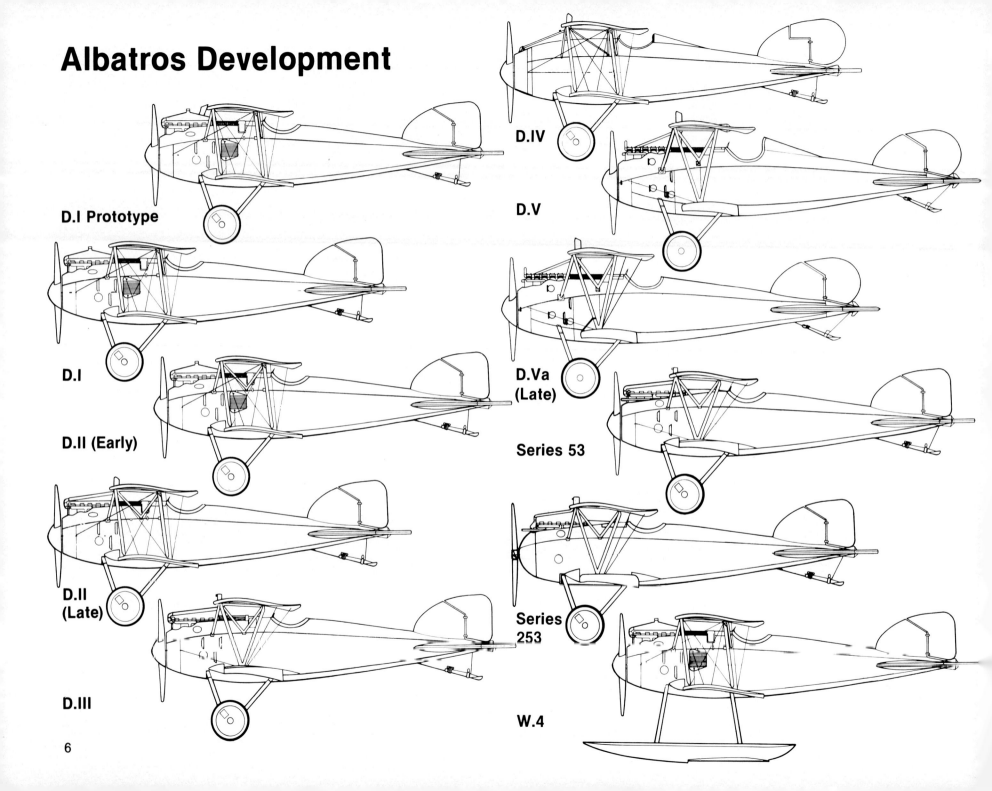

D.I Prototype

D.I

D.II (Early)

D.II (Late)

D.III

D.IV

D.V

D.Va (Late)

Series 53

Series 253

W.4

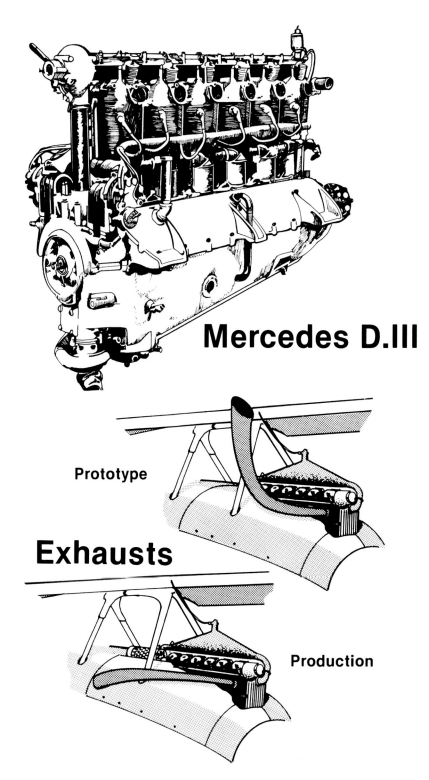

Mercedes D.III

Exhausts

Prototype

Production

Line-up of Albatros D.Is of Boelcke's Jasta 2 at Berthincourt, September 1916.

At times, fighter aircraft were assigned to bomber and reconnaissance units for escort or liason duty, like this D.I which served with Kampfgeschwader V, Staffel 15. Position of upper wing, which limited upward visibility, is apparent.

A D.I of Kampfein-sitzerstaffel (KEST) Morchingen, **a home defense unit.**

391/16, a D.I flown by Lt. Büttner of Jasta 2 was brought down intact by the British in December 1916 and extensively tested and studied. This aircraft was one of the twelve pre produotion D.Is ordered in June 1916.

The Albatros D.II

The Albatros **D.II** was developed to correct some of the design flaws of the D.I. The upper wing of the D.I was mounted in such a way as to restrict the pilot's vision forward and upward. Sighting forward through the legs of the one-piece cabane structure was difficult. Additionally, the fuselage-mounted radiators, besides being a detriment to the aircraft's streamlining, created another problem. When punctured by a bullet, their positioning would allow water to drain from the cylinder heads, resulting in engine seizure.

On the Albatros D.II, the trestle cabane structure was replaced by a pair of splayed 'N'-struts, which allowed the lowering of the upper wing. This improved forward visibility considerably. It also allowed for a Teeves and Braun radiator to be mounted in the upper wing center-section, although many early D.IIs still carried the fuselage-mounted Windhoff radiators. (It is assumed, therefore, that these initial D.IIs were in fact built as D.Is but, when assembled, incorporated the newer strut arrangement and were thus designated as D.IIs.) The wing-mounted radiator did much to clean up the appearance of the aircraft, but it created a combat hazard of its own. If the radiator were holed by a bullet, the pilot could be sprayed in the face with scalding water.

Since production of the D.II followed so closely upon that of the D.I, the two aircraft made their combat debuts at about the same time. One D.II was reported in service in September 1916; 28 were at the front in November and, in January 1917, the D.II's service peak, 214 were in combat use. A total of 275 D.IIs were built, 200 by the parent Albatros company and 75 under contract by L.V.G. (*Luft Verkehrs Gesellschaft*).

The D.II showed no real increase in performance over the D.I. In fact, its climb to 1,000 meters took 50 seconds longer, and its combat endurance was an hour and a half — 20 minutes less than the D.I. Top speed was the same, but the D.II's service ceiling of 5,200 meters (17,060ft) was 200 meters higher than that of the D.I.

Albatros D.II prototype with upper wing in the lowered position caused by the new cabane system. Note non-standard windscreen. As on D.I prototype, no armament was carried.

A flight of four Albatros D.IIs.

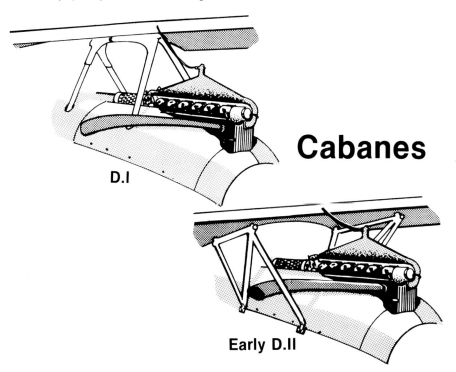

Cabanes

D.I

Early D.II

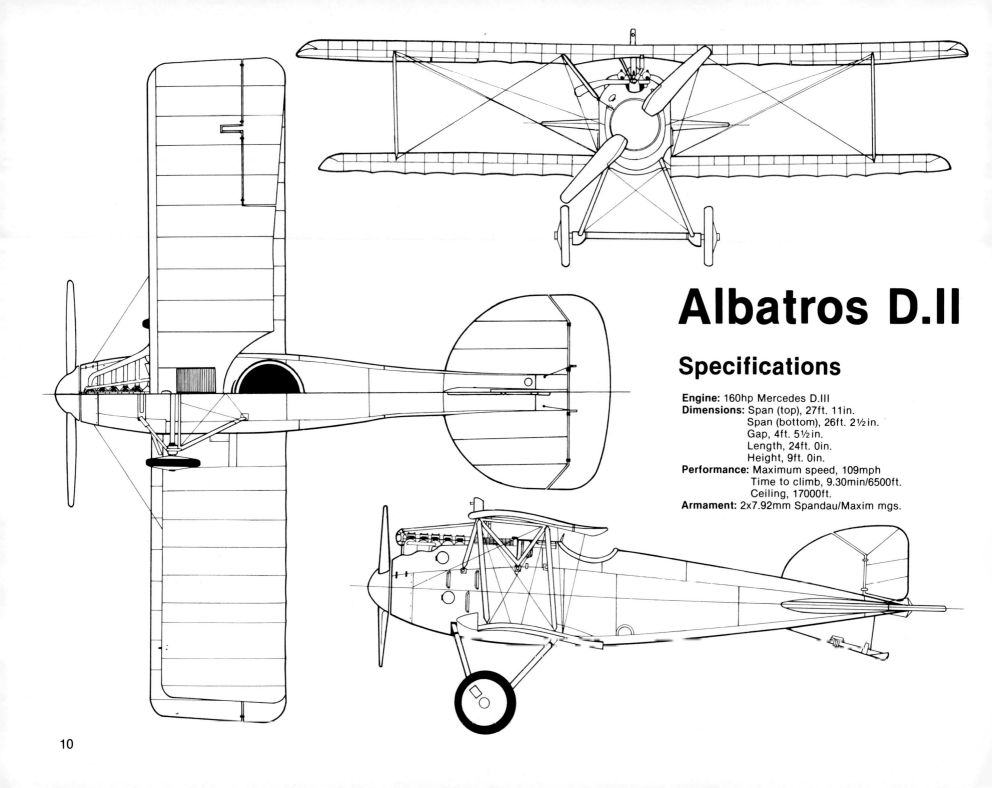

Albatros D.II

Specifications

Engine: 160hp Mercedes D.III
Dimensions: Span (top), 27ft. 11in.
             Span (bottom), 26ft. 2½in.
             Gap, 4ft. 5½in.
             Length, 24ft. 0in.
             Height, 9ft. 0in.
Performance: Maximum speed, 109mph
             Time to climb, 9.30min/6500ft.
             Ceiling, 17000ft.
Armament: 2x7.92mm Spandau/Maxim mgs.

Albatros aircraft of Jasta 4 at Hivry-Cricourt during the winter of 1916-17.

(Above Right) Lt. Kralewski's nosed over Albatros D.II of Jasta 4 shows position of wing-mounted Teeves & Braun radiator. National markings with thin white outline became standard in late 1916. Wing colors are green (light area) and chestnut brown (dark area).

Radiators

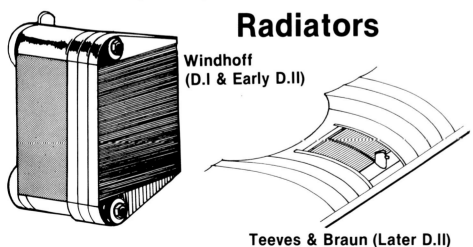

Windhoff
(D.I & Early D.II)

Teeves & Braun (Later D.II)

Pilots and mechanics of Jasta 10 pose with Lt. Alois Heldmann's over-turned D.II. Heldmann (third from left) appears uninjured by the accident. With his arm around Heldmann is Vfw. Barth.

(Above and Below) Early Albatros D.IIs retained the fuselage-mounted Windhoff radiators, like this RAF-captured example.

Albatros D.II, serial D.1782/16, the 83rd aircraft of the second D.II production batch of 100 ordered in September 1916. Pilot is unidentified. (Air Force Museum)

The great Oswald Boelcke (second from right) being congratulated on this 34th victory. He would attain six more before being killed on 28 October 1916, the result of a collision with one of his own pilots during a dogfight. The first aerial tactician, he was respected by his enemies as well as his comrades. Several German aces would become successful because of Boelcke's leadership, including leading ace Manfred von Richthofen. After Boelcke's death, Jasta 2 was renamed Jasta Boelcke by Imperial Decree.

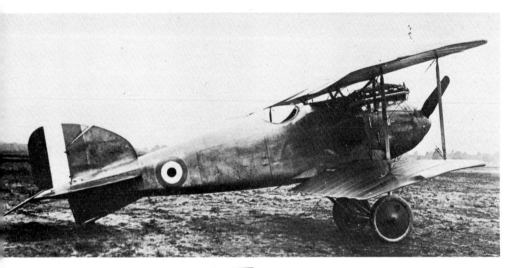

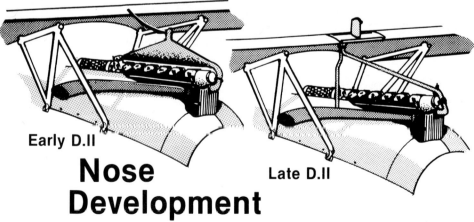

Early D.II

Nose Development

Late D.II

The Albatros D.III

The Albatros **D.III** was an attempt to improve the maneuverability of the D.II. In this, Thelen and his design team were influenced by the French Nieuport fighters and their rather unusual wing layout. The Nieuport was not a true biplane, but rather a "sesquiplane", having a wing-and-a-half instead of two. The lower wing, built around a single spar, was of much narrower chord than the upper, with interplane bracing being achieved by 'V'-struts. This arrangement provided good maneuverability and excellent downward vision. Captured Nieuports were sent to all major German aircraft firms, including Albatros, with the hope that some of the Nieuport's features could be incorporated into a German fighter and favorable results achieved.

Thelen and his staff designed a new wing cellule based on the sesquiplane idea. The lower wing was of less chord than the upper, but not quite so radically as that of the Nieuport's. The tips of both wings were raked, and the parallel interplane struts were replaced with a single 'V'-strut on each side. This new wing structure was combined with the existing D.II fuselage, the resulting aircraft being designated the Albatros D.III.

The new wing plan gave the D.III improved maneuverability and rate of climb, but there was no appreciable increase in speed over the D.II. The D.III could reach 1,000 meters in two and a half minutes, and flight endurance was increased to two hours.

As with later D.IIs, the D.III featured a Teeves and Braun radiator in the upper wing center section. In later D.IIIs, the radiator was moved from the middle to the starboard side of the center section to minimize the danger of pilot scalding if the radiator was punctured by a bullet. The relocation of the radiator, and the resulting rearrangement of the radiator piping, also helped improve vision.

The D.III had one serious drawback. In adopting the Nieuport wing plan, the Albatros inherited the French fighter's chief weakness. The single-spar lower wing had a tendency to collapse under the stress of a prolonged dive or excessive maneuvers. Several German aviators experienced wing failures, including leading ace Manfred von Richthofen, who gave up the Albatros for about a month and flew a Halberstadt D.II instead. He later returned to flying the Albatros, perhaps believing the risks of its structural weaknesses were outweighed by its excellent performance.

At any rate, the D.III was still far superior to any Allied fighter of the time, a fact which contributed to the severe losses suffered by the British during the so-called 'Bloody April' of 1917. During that month, the British lost 151 aircraft on the Western Front, while bringing down only 30 German aircraft. The end of April, however, saw the introduction of newer and better British aircraft, such as the Royal Aircraft Factory S.E.5, which helped bring about an end to the Albatros' superiority.

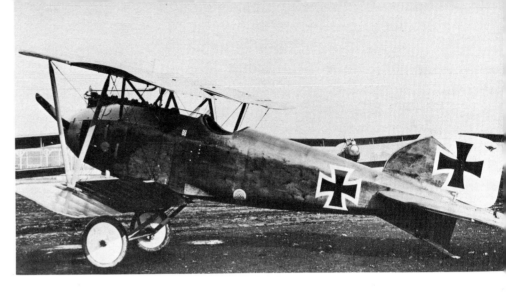

Albatros D.III prototype. Fuselage appears to be covered in a dark wood stain instead of clear varnish. Albatros trademark is apparent on clear-doped rudder. Note narrow-chord lower wing and 'V'-shaped interplane struts.

Deliveries of the Albatros D.III began in December 1916, and thirteen examples of the type were in service by the end of the following month. There were 137 in service by March, 327 by May. The D.III's service peak came in November 1917, when there were 446 examples at the front. A total of 1,340 Albatros D.IIIs were built, 500 by the parent firm at Johannistahl, and 840 by the *Ostdeutsche Albatros Werke (O.A.W.),* the company's East German branch at Schneidemuhl. *O.A.W.*-built D.IIIs were largely similar to those built at Johannistahl, but featured a larger rudder with a fully rounded trailing edge.

D.III was quite possibly the best looking of the Albatros fighter series, a fact borne out by this example, set against a winter background.

Wing Tips & Struts

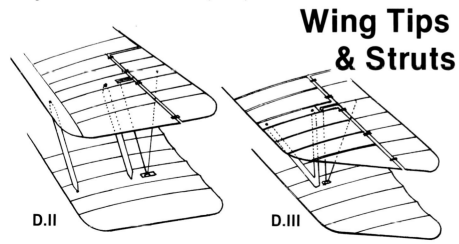

D.II   D.III

Albatros D.IIs and D.IIIs of Jasta 5 at Boistrancourt, April 1917. Note different styles of national markings. Individual markings were black and white.

Radiators

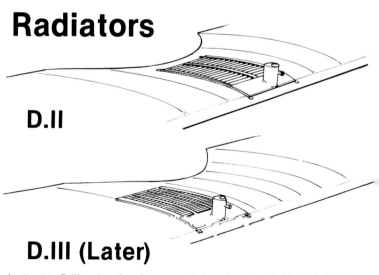

D.II

D.III (Later)

Jasta 14 D.IIIs. In the foreground is aircraft of Lt. Friedrich Vonschoot. Veltjen's machine is in background. Note absence of prop spinners. Photo taken probably in April 1917.

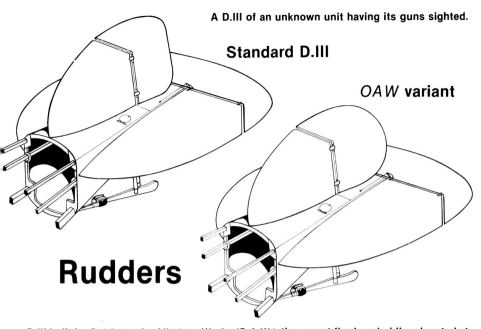

Standard D.III

OAW variant

A D.III of an unknown unit having its guns sighted.

Rudders

D.III built by *Ostdeutsche Albatros Werke (O.A.W.)*, the parent firm's subsidiary located at Schneidemuhl, is characterized by its curved rudder.

An *O.A.W.*-built D.III over the Russian Front. Dark green and mauve camouflage on upper wing is apparent, as is radiator located on starboard side of wing center section.

(Above Left) In all wars, on all fronts, maintenance is an endless task. Here, mechanics of Jasta 29 replace the propeller of a D.III after working on its engine.

Overturned D.III assigned to Flieger Abteilung (A) 250 at Heule vividly demonstrates weakness of lower wing. Wing failures like this were to plague Albatros D.IIIs, and later D.Vs, throughout their service careers. The single spar, around which the lower wing was built, could break under stress of excessive maneuvers or prolonged dives.

D.IIIs of Jasta 29. Aircraft No. 2 was flown by Lt. Wilhelm Almenröder, No. 4 by Corp. Fritzsche. Numerals are black with white outline. Note difference in fuselage coloration; aircraft No. 2 was coated in dark stain, No. 4 in clear varnish.

Only late in the war were German pilots equipped with parachutes. Here, a pilot of Jasta 8 is helped into his harness. The parachute pack lies atop fuselage. Note flare cartridge rack on fuselage side and the rear-view mirror on the wing.

Albatros D.IIs and D.IIIs of Jasta 10 at Ancervilles, Spring 1917.

Vfw. Barth's D.III of Jasta 10 is easily pushed into its hangar. Aircraft of this unit had yellow noses, white personal markings and black numerals.

Lt. Karl Allmenröder of Jasta 11 in his D.III. This aircraft had a red fuselage, tail, undercarriage and struts. Nose and elevators were white. A 30-victory ace, Allmenroder was shot down and killed on 27 June 1917 by Canadian ace Raymond Collishaw.

Lt. von Budde of Jasta 29 in his D.III, serial D.2052/16. Note large windscreen. The personal initial is black and white.

Lt. Kurt Student, CO of Jasta 9, in his D.III which also is fitted with a non-standard windscreen. Student gained nine victories, survived the war and served with distinction in the Luftwaffe during WWII.

Pilots and mechanics of Jasta 26 discuss ways of righting Lt. Bruno Lörzer's black-and-white striped D.III. Note fabric repair patch on port upper wingtip, central location of wing radiator and green/brown upper wing camouflage pattern.

Lt. Kurt Schneider of Jasta 5 poses with the unit mascot in front of his D.III. The 15-victory ace acted as CO of Jasta 5 from 4-20 May 1917, but was killed in action on 5 June.

Lt. Alfred Lenz seated in his Albatros D.III which he flew while with Jasta 14 during the spring of 1917. Lenz became CO of Jasta 22 on 21 July 1917, gaining six victories before war's end.

A D.III of Jasta 29. This aircraft was part of the third and last production batch built at Johannistahl, ordered in March 1917. Radiator is offset to starboard. Note the common German habit of repeating the aircraft number on the aircraft's spine.

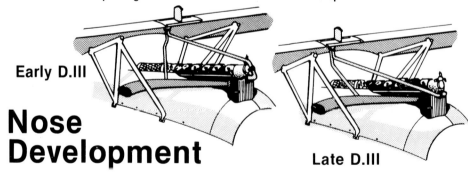

Early D.III

Nose
Development

Late D.III

The Albatros D.III remained in front-line service much longer than is generally believed. This example, photographed in May 1918 was flown by Lt. Franz Ray, CO of Jasta 49. Aircraft has a black fuselage, white fin and rudder. Wings are covered in the then-standard five-color lozenge camouflage fabric highlighted by light blue rib tapes. Note the straight-armed *Balkenkreuz* which replaced the *Pathe'* cross in early 1918. This example is most unusual in having a small airfoil fitted over its landing gear axle.

The Albatros D.IV

The Albatros **D.IV** was developed in late 1916 as a test bed for an experimental, geared version of the Mercedes engine. It was not, as previously thought, intended as a replacement for the Albatros D.III.

Three D.IVs were ordered, but probably only one was built. The fuselage was similar to that of the D.I-D.III series, but featured a small headrest for the pilot, and the engine was completely enclosed in the fuselage nose. Wing construction returned to the two-spar lower plane and parallel interplane struts of the D.I and D.II. The tail plane was of a narrower chord than the previous fighters, and the rudder featured a square rather than a triangular balance.

The performance of the D.IV was poor, largely due to teething problems with the geared Mercedes. Testing with the aircraft, using various types of propellers, continued until at least April 1918.

The only verified Albatros D.IV prototype. Note small headrest, square balance on rudder, larger chord of lower wing, parallel interplane struts and completely cowled engine. Of three examples ordered, this is probably the only one completed.

The Albatros D.V and D.Va

In developing a successor to the Albatros D.III, Thelen and his staff decided to design a new fuselage and retain the wing plan of the D.III. The Albatros **D.V**, therefore, featured a fuselage that was completely oval in cross-section, in contrast to the flat-sided fuselage of the D.I-D.III series. The lower wing root was not faired into the fuselage structure as on the previous fighters. Instead, the lower wing planes were attached to small stubs mounted on the lower fuselage sides. A rather high headrest was fitted to the D.V, which was often removed in service as it seriously obstructed rearward vision. On later D.Vs, the headrest was eliminated in production.

The tail unit of the D.III was retained on the D.V, but included the larger, curved rudder fitted to O.A.W.-built aircraft. The underfin of the D.V had a more raked appearance. The wings of the D.V were identical in construction and dimension to those of the D.III, but differed in the method of aileron control. On the D.III, the control cables came down from the aileron, entered the lower wing near the base of the 'V'-strut, then continued through the lower wing to the control column, then down into the fuselage. The cables on the D.V passed through the upper wing, then down into the fuselage.

The Albatros **D.Va** was developed soon after the D.V. It featured a strengthened airframe, which brought the empty weight to 1580 lbs, as opposed to 1500 lbs for the D.V. It was powered by a more powerful version of the Mercedes D.III, uprated to 180hp. The most apparent difference was the aileron control, the D.Va reverting back to the system of the D.III, perhaps because a more positive control response was achieved. In fact, the

The prototype Albatros D.V was completely covered in five-color lozenge camouflage, including metal panels and struts. The prototype's rudder has straight trailing edge of D.I-D.III series. This aircraft was being test-flown by April 1917.

Aft Fuselage

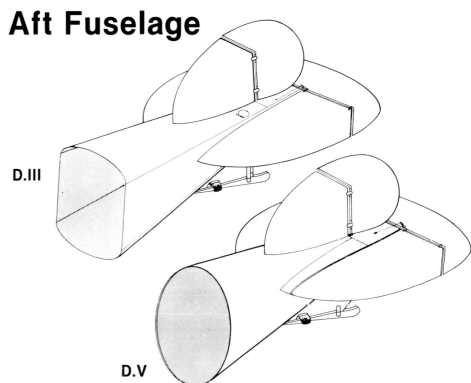

D.III

D.V

wings of the D.III and D.Va were interchangeable.

The Albatros D.V began to enter service in May 1917, the D.Va in October. Their performance was only slightly better than the D.III's, with a top speed of about 106mph and climb to 1,000 meters taking four minutes and 20 seconds. Therefore, German pilots expecting an improvement over the D.III were very disappointed. Current Allied aircraft were more than a match for the D.V and D.Va.

In addition, the wing structural problems that had plagued the D.III were not eliminated in the D.V. One pilot, Lt. Von Hippel of **Jasta 5**, lost the entire left lower wing of his D.V during a dogfight on 5 February 1918. Von Hippel managed to bring the aircraft under control, but overturned on landing at Le Catelet. Miraculously, he was uninjured, but was understandably shaken by the incident.

Investigation into this and other D.V wing failures found that the problem lay mostly in faulty design of the spar attachment system. A stronger one was designed and replaced on aircraft in the field. Other modifications fitted to D.Vs and D.Vas included an extra bracing wire from the fuselage nose to the point of the 'V'-strut, and to the top rear leg of the strut. Also, a small auxiliary strut was attached from the front leg of the 'V'-strut to the lower wing leading edge. Even with these modifications, pilots were urged not to over-dive their Albatros and to avoid overzealous maneuvers.

Even though it was more or less obsolete when it entered service, the Albatros D.V/Va could, in the hands of a skilled pilot, give a good account of itself in combat. It bore the brunt of the aerial fighting that took place during the German Offensive of 1918, and several well-known aces such as Manfred von Richthofen, Hermann Göring, Bruno Lörzer, Erich Löwenhardt and Edouard von Schleich made extensive use of the aircraft.

The D.V/Va was the most produced and widely used of all the Albatros fighters, a total of 2,512 (900 D.Vs, 1,612 D.Vas) having been built. At their service peak in May 1918, there were 1,117 of these types at the front — 131 D.Vs and 986 D.Vas. With the arrival of the excellent Fokker D.VII in the Spring of 1918, the number of Albatros D.Vs and D.Vas began to decline, but the type remained in wide service with German air units until the Armistice.

Fin Development

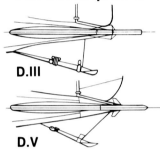

D.III

D.V

Albatros D.V serial D.1021/17, the twenty-second D.V built of the first production batch (200), ordered in April 1917. The high headrest is apparent. This blocked rear vision, causing its removal from many aircraft in service.

Cockpit & Headrest Development

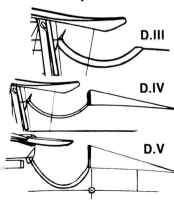

D.III

D.IV

D.V

Groundcrewmen of Jasta 10 pose with that unit's D.Vs at Marcke, Belgium, summer 1917. Aircraft shown are those flown by (l. to r.) Heldmann, Löwenhardt, Barth, Weigand, Aue, Burgaller and Kuhn. All aircraft had yellow noses with white personal markings.

Wing Root

D.III Faired

D.V Not Faired

D.IIIs and D.Vs of Jasta 12. Black tails and white spinners were a feature of this unit. Personal markings were black and white. Two aircraft in foreground were flown by Hptm. Adolf Ritter von Tutschek, CO of the *staffel*.

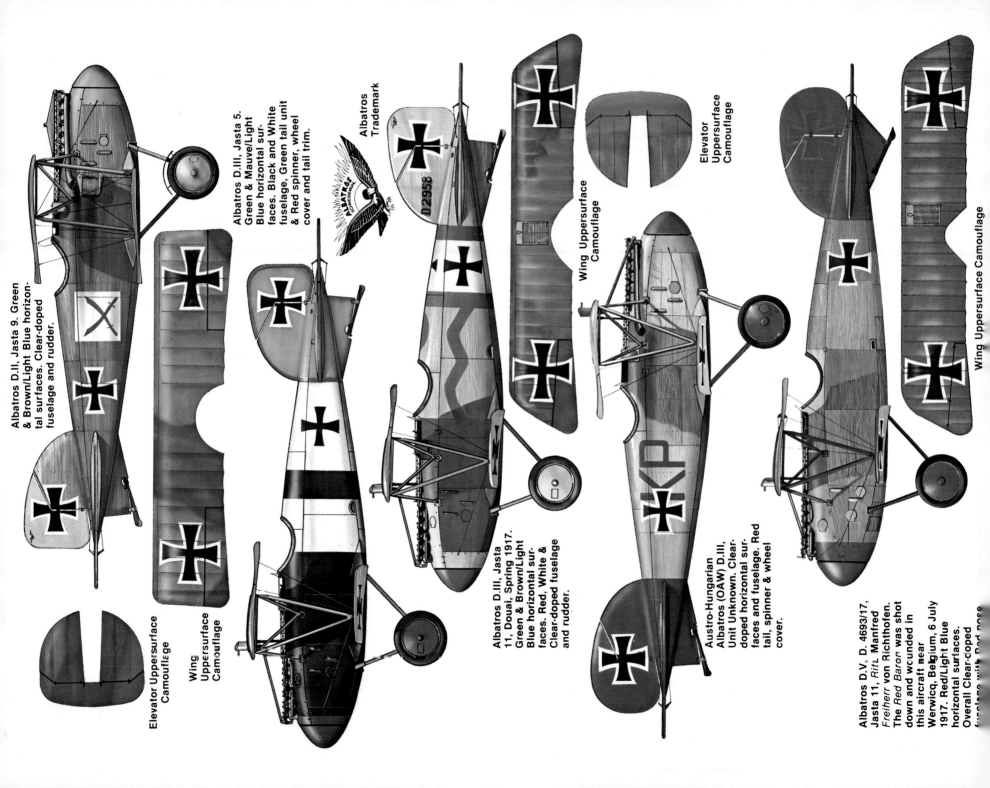

Albatros D.II, Jasta 9. Green & Brown/Light Blue horizontal surfaces. Clear-doped fuselage and rudder.

Elevator Uppersurface Camouflage

Wing Uppersurface Camouflage

Albatros D.III, Jasta 5. Green & Mauve/Light Blue horizontal surfaces. Black and White fuselage, Green tail unit & Red spinner, wheel cover and tail trim.

Albatros Trademark

Albatros D.III, Jasta 11, Douai, Spring 1917. Green & Brown/Light Blue horizontal surfaces. Red, White & Clear-doped fuselage and rudder.

D2958

Wing Uppersurface Camouflage

Elevator Uppersurface Camouflage

Austro-Hungarian Albatros (OAW) D.III, Unit Unknown. Clear-doped horizontal surfaces and fuselage. Red tail, spinner & wheel cover.

Wing Uppersurface Camouflage

Albatros D.V. D. 4693/17, Jasta 11, *Ritt.* Manfred *Frhr.* von Richthofen. The *Red Baron* was shot down and wcunded in this aircraft near Werwicq, Belgium, 6 July 1917. Red/Light Blue horizontal surfaces. Overall Clear-coped

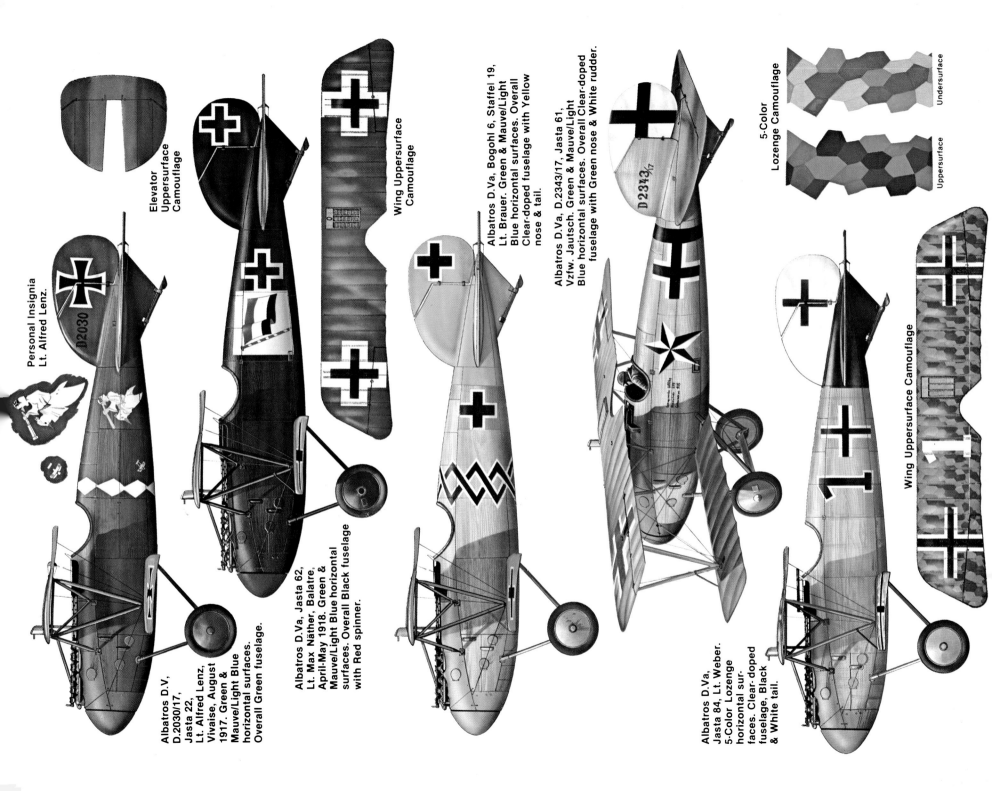

Personal Insignia Lt. Alfred Lenz.

Elevator Uppersurface Camouflage

Wing Uppersurface Camouflage

5-Color Lozenge Camouflage

Undersurface

Uppersurface

Uppersurface

Wing Uppersurface Camouflage

Albatros D.V., D.2030/17, Jasta 22, Lt. Alfred Lenz, Vivaise, August 1917. Green & Mauve/Light Blue horizontal surfaces. Overall Green fuselage.

Albatros D.Va, Jasta 62, Lt. Max Näther, Balatre, April-May 1918. Green & Mauve/Light Blue horizontal surfaces. Overall Black fuselage with Red spinner.

Albatros D.Va, Bogohl 6, Staffel 19, Lt. Brauer. Green & Mauve/Light Blue horizontal surfaces. Overall Clear-doped fuselage with Yellow nose & tail.

Albatros D.Va, D.2343/17, Jasta 61, Vzfw. Jautsch. Green & Mauve/Light Blue horizontal surfaces. Overall Clear-doped fuselage with Green nose & White rudder.

Albatros D.Va, Jasta 84, Lt. Weber. 5-Color Lozenge horizontal surfaces. Clear-doped fuselage, Black & White tail.

Pilots and Albatros D.Vs of *Jasta 37*. Aircraft in foreground, serial D.4427/17, with the black and white star marking, is personal machine of Oblt. Hans Waldhausen, who is seated at the right bottom playing chess.

A stretcher being prepared for the wounded pilot of D.V, serial D.1066/17.

Control Arm Shroud

The wing structural failures that had plagued the Albatros D.III recurred in the D.V, as evidenced here. Only the pressure of war can explain the fact that the D.V was ordered into full-scale production before its cause was determined and this problem was rectified. Note aileron control arm shrouds, a common feature in the D.V.

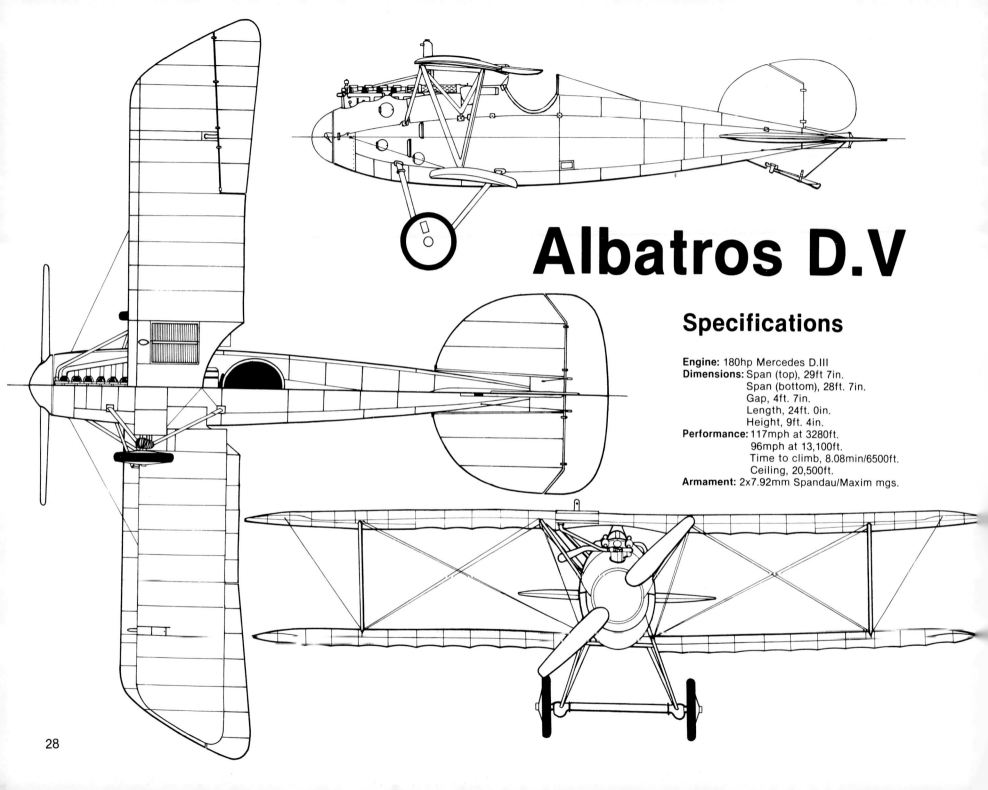

Albatros D.V

Specifications

Engine: 180hp Mercedes D.III
Dimensions: Span (top), 29ft 7in.
Span (bottom), 28ft. 7in.
Gap, 4ft. 7in.
Length, 24ft. 0in.
Height, 9ft. 4in.
Performance: 117mph at 3280ft.
96mph at 13,100ft.
Time to climb, 8.08min/6500ft.
Ceiling, 20,500ft.
Armament: 2x7.92mm Spandau/Maxim mgs.

Line-up of garishly marked D.Vs of Jasta 5 at Boistran-court, January 1918. All aircraft of this unit had green tails, outlined in red, with red spinners and wheels. Aircraft at far left is Lt. Paul Baumer's. Fifth machine from left is Von Hippel's.

Albatros D.Vs of Jasta 32b at Chery-les-Pouilly, October 1917. Aircraft in foreground is that of the unit's CO. Oblt. Eduard Ritter von Schleich. His machine had all-black fuselage, tail and wheel covers, white spinner, lozenge camouflage wings.

D.Vs of Jasta 22 at Mout, August 1917. Machine in rear is Lt. Wunsch's.

Lt. Hans Joachim von Hippel's D.V overturned at Le Catelet, 18 February 1918, after losing its port lower wing during a dogfight at 15,000 ft. Von Hippel regained control long enough to land and, miraculously, survived unhurt. Luckily, he had been flying a D.V, on which the aileron control cables ran through the upper wing, rather than the later D.Va with cables through the lower wing.

This D.Va with skull and crossbones markings was captured and tested by the French. A look at the lower wing will show that the light blue center to the French roundel is there. It has dropped out on the side and tail due to the brightness of the sun and the use of orthochromatic film which lightens blue.

(Right & Below) D.V, serial 4545/17, flown by Vzfw. Max Wachwitz of Jasta 24, was brought down intact by ground fire near Bethune on 7 December 1917. It was test flown by the British. Note five-color lozenge camouflage on wings and tailplane. The fuselage and tail are varnished plywood. Aircraft in backgound are Royal Aircraft Factory B.E.2cs.

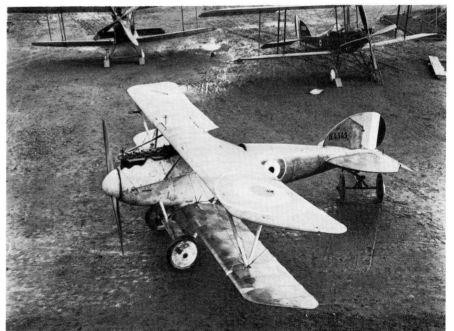

Albatros D.IIIs, D.Vs, and, in the foreground, a Roland D.II of Lt. Hermann Göring's Jasta 27.

Lt. Carl Menckhoff with his D.V of Jasta 3 at Rumbeke, August 1917. An ace with 39 victories, Menckhoff became CO of Jasta 72 on 23 April 1918. He was shot down on 25 July by Lt. Walter Avery of the US Air Service and made prisoner. The fuselage is camouflaged, probably in green and mauve, in similar fashion to the wings. Undersides are believed to be light blue. Menckhoff's initial on side is black, the wheels white.

D.V Cockpit

1. Fuel Gauge
2. Tachometer
3. Compass
4. Fuel Pressure Gauge
5. Floor
6. Water Pump (greaser)
7. Fuel Pump (hand)
8. Main Throttle
9. Control Stick
10. Auxiliary Throttle
11. Spark Control
12. Magneto
13. Hand-Cranked Magneto (for starting)
14. Rudder Pedals
15. Triggers

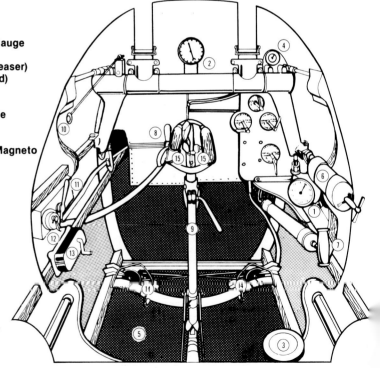

D.Vs and D.Vas of Marine Feld Jasta 2, led by Lt. Theo Osterkamp at Jabbecke.

Oblt. Bruno Lörzer, CO of Jasta 26, talks to Crown Prince Wilhelm from the cockpit of his black and white striped D.V. Lörzer survived the war with 41 victories and served in the *Luftwaffe* in WWII. (Air Force Museum)

Another view of Jasta 32b. The second aircraft, with the black and white circle on the fuselage, was flown by Vzfw. Paul Retsch. All aircraft of this unit have black tails.

A D.V of a German Naval unit which apparently had a rough landing on the beach at Ostende, Belgium. The fuselage band is black and white, the tail red.

Experimental gun mounting on the upper wing of an Albatros D.V using a captured Lewis gun.

Spandau/Maxim

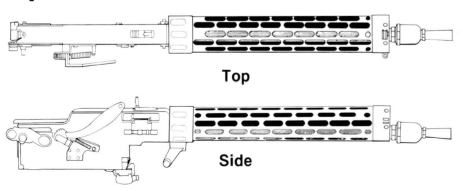

Top

Side

(Right Above & Right) Another experimental gun mount, this one featuring an Italian Villar-Perosa gun. Many of these two-barreled, 9mm weapons were captured at Caporetto in late 1917. Unfortunately, it didn't have enough striking power for effective aerial use.

A D.V with stylized cross on fuselage and rudder. For some reason, fuselage cross has been painted out and remarked further forward. (Peter M. Bowers)

(Left & Below) *O.A.W.*-built D.Va, serial A.W.S. D.6988/17, possibly of Jasta 78b, was interned in Switzerland after the pilot became lost. The aircraft carries late-style German national markings, introduced in June 1918. The view below shows the aircraft after its rudder and fuselage crosses have been painted out, the latter seemingly replaced with a Swiss white cross. Initials A.W.S. in serial stood for *Albatroswerke Schneidemuhl* another name for *Ostdeutsche Albatros Werke.*

The Austrian Albatroses

The Albatros D.II and D.III were produced in Austria by the *Oesterreichische Flugzeugfabrik A.G. (Oeffag)* of Wiener-Neustadt and saw much service with the **Königlich und Kaiserlich Luftfahrtruppen** (Royal and Imperial Air Service) of the Austro-Hungarian Army. These aircraft were built in three series, serialed 53, 153 and 253. (Each Austrian aircraft manufacturer was assigned a key digit: in the case of *Oeffag*, this digit was 5. Another digit designated the specific aircraft type, the Albatros being assigned the digit 3. If more than one series of an aircraft type was produced, a third key digit, in sequence, was added to the **front** of the serial, hence 53, 153 and 253 for the three series of the Albatros. These three key digits were followed by a decimal point, and after that the number of the individual aircraft in the series. Thus, the serial 153.25 on the side of an aircraft indicates that it is the twenty-fifth Albatros of the second production series.)

In most respects, the Austrian Albatroses resembled their German counterparts. There were differences, however, principally in power and armament. Power was supplied by the excellent Austro-Daimler engine in three power ratings: 185hp (Series 53), 200hp (Series 153) and 225hp (Series 253). Armament consisted of twin, synchronized Schwarzlose machine guns which were completely buried under the fuselage decking, and fired through long blast tubes on either side of the engine cylinder banks. (Only one gun was fitted to the D.II version.) The Schwarzlose was of Austrian manufacture and was not as reliable as the German Maxim. It had a slower rate of fire and was prone to jamming.

The first 16 aircraft of the 53 Series were built as Albatros D.IIs, the remainder of all three Series were D.IIIs. In the 253 Series, the use of the largest and most powerful Austro-Daimler engine necessitated some modification to the aircraft's nose, eliminating the propeller spinner.

It is a credit to *Oeffag's* designers that the Austrian Albatros D.IIIs did not exhibit the wing structural problems of their German counterparts. This is because the Austrian engineers took special pains to strengthen the wing structure at the leading edge and strut attachment points.

The *Oeffag* Albatros was perhaps the best single-seater used by the Austro-Hungarian Air Service, and they were well-liked by their pilots. Several Austro-Hungarian aces, such as Godwin Brumowski, Frank Linke-Crawford and Josef Kiss flew the Albatros during their combat careers and gained several victories mounting it.

Production of the *Oeffag* Albatros began in January 1917, and continued until October 1918, with a total of about 540 aircraft being completed. The most produced variant was the 153 Series, 286 of which were built.

First *Oeffag*-built Albatros D.II, serial 53.01, of Austro-Hungarian Air Service. Note the wind-driven Anomometer attached to left forward interplane strut. The only paint applied to the prototype was the national markings and serial numbers. Wings, tail plane and rudder were clear doped, fuselage clear varnished, cowl panels, spinner and inspection plates bare metal.

Armament

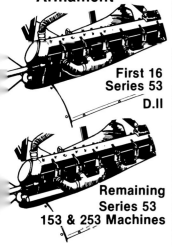

First 16
Series 53
D.II

Remaining
Series 53
153 & 253 Machines

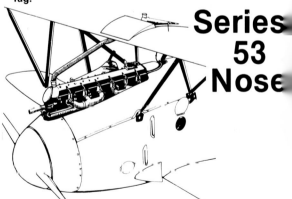

D.II serial 53.15 was next-to-last D.II built by Oeffag.

Series 53 Nose

Oeffag-built D.III 53.24 was fifth D.III of the series (serials for D.III variants had begun with 53.20). Power plant was 185hp Austro-Daimler, which gave aircraft a top speed of about 110mph. Rate of climb was also slightly superior to German D.III.

Flamboyant color schemes were not often found on Austro-Hungarian aircraft, although some personal markings did appear, such as this black and white geometric design on 53.27, believed flown by Gottfried *Freiherr* von Banfield.

The second-highest scoring Austro-Hungarian ace was Julius Arigi, shown here in his Albatros D.III. Arigi attained 32 victories becoming the most-decorated NCO in the Austrian *Luftfahrtruppen*. During WWII he served as a *Luftwaffe* flying instructor and counted aces Walter Nowotny and Hans-Joachim Marseille among his pupils.

D.III, serial 53.40, flown by Oblt. Fischer cracked up during landing, having apparently hit the ditch shown. Blast tubes of buried Schwarzlose guns can be seen at sides of engine cylinder bank. Also note the shaped aluminum fairings which streamline the wing root into the contours of the lower fuselage.

D.III, 53.38, in flight over the Alps. The war in the air between the Austro-Hungarians and the Italians was fought over some of the world's most rugged terrain. This was the 19th D.III of the 53 Series, out of a total of 44. This aircraft appears to be fitted with an auxiliary strut from the lower wing leading edge to front interplane strut leg in the manner of the German Albatros D.Va. Austrian D.IIIs, however, were never plagued with the wing structural problems which characterized the German.

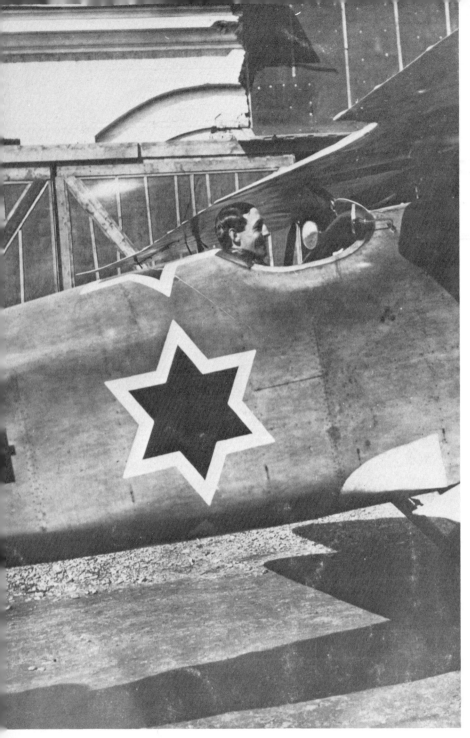

Motor von D.3.

(Above) the engine mount of an Austrian D.III shows the blast tube for one of the buried guns. Also note piping for the wing-mounted radiator.

(Left) An unidentified Austro-Hungarian pilot with black and white Star of David personal mark. Note the twin rear-view mirrors on either side of the cockpit and the small windscreen.

(Right) Cockpit of Austrian D.III.

With the availability of the 200hp Austro-Daimler, production of the 153 Series Albatros began, the first examples ready for service use by July 1917. Shown is the seventh production machine. A total of 281 D.IIIs were built in this series.

In-flight photo of the D.III that belonged to ace Frank Linke-Crawford.

Last production variant of Austrian D.III was the 253 Series, powered by 225hp Austro-Daimler. Use of this more powerful engine necessitated the modification of the nose, including the sacrifice of the propeller spinner. 201 aircraft were built in this series, the first examples being delivered in May 1918.

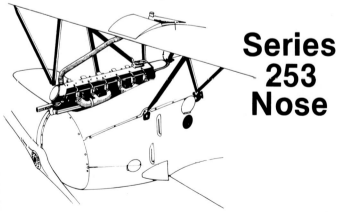

Series 253 Nose

D.III, serial 253.238, possibly of Flik 32, with interesting personal marking, a striped fin.

Line-up of some variously damaged Austrian Albatros fighters at an airfield in Northern Italy.

(Right & Below) Wrecked Austrian D.III-type aircraft abandoned at Gorizia railway station by the retreating Austro-Hungarians.

Albatros W.4 prototype, serial 747, ordered in June 1916 and completed three months later. It is seen in these three views being examined by German Naval personnel. Note the square-section floats, characteristic of early versions.

The Albatros W.4

The Albatros **W.4** was developed in response to a German Admiralty request for a high performance seaplane to protect its bases along the Flanders Coast. The first W.4 was ordered in June 1916 and delivered in September. It resembled the D.I landplane, then in production at Johannistahl, but had larger wings with increased gap. Fin and rudder area was also increased, and the fuselage underfin eliminated.

Only the prototype W.4 was built by the Albatros company. The rest were constructed by the seaplane works at Friedrichshagen, a suburb of Berlin. Later W.4s featured floats of better aerodynamic shape, shorter float struts, a wing-mounted radiator and ailerons on both wings.

The W.4 showed excellent performance for a seaplane, with a top speed of about 100mph. It could climb to 3,000 meters (9,840ft) in 11½ minutes, and its maneuverability was also good.

A total of 118 W.4s were built, in eight production batches, and deliveries took place between September 1916 and December 1917. It was used mostly on the Baltic and North Sea coasts by the German Navy. Eight second-hand W.4s were obtained by the Austro-Hungarian Naval Air Service and operated in the Aegean. The W.4 remained in service until the Armistice. At war's end, 67 were still listed as being in service use.

Albatros W.4 serial 1486 illustrates features of late production aircraft of this type, notably more aerodynamic floats, shorter float struts, wing-mounted radiator and ailerons on both wings. This aircraft appears to be unarmed.

(Above, Left & Left Below) Albatros W.4 in flight shows its clean lines to good advantage.

German Naval mechanics at work on a W.4 during the spring of 1918. (Peter M. Bowers)

48

Adolf Blaha, a Czechoslovakian pilot who flew with the Austro-Hungarian *Luftfahrtruppen* poses with his Albatros at Zurich, Switzerland, in February 1919. Blaha had become lost in fog during a flight on 22 October 1918, landed at Zurich, and was interned for the last few days of the war along with his aircraft. Serial of this machine was 253.116. After the independence of Czechoslovakia was established, Blaha was allowed to fly his aircraft home.

Post-War Albatros

The combat career of the Albatros did not end with the closing of World War One. A large number of Austrian-built D.IIIs, mostly of the 253 Series, were obtained by Poland after the Armistice and were an important component in the formation of the Polish Air Force. The Polish D.IIIs saw extensive service during the Polish-Russian War of 1919-20. The most illustrious user of the aircraft was the famed **Eskadra Kosciuszkowska**

(Kosciuszko Squadron), a group of American volunteers organized shortly after the Armistice by Capt. Merian C. Cooper and Maj. Cedric E. Fauntleroy.

Combat in Poland consisted mostly of ground attack, due to the lack of Russian aerial opposition. The armament officer of the Kosciuszko Squadron, Maj. Edward W. Chess, modified the firing mechanism of the aircrafts' guns and doubled the rate of fire from 100 to 200 rounds per minute. Racks for small bombs were fitted to the wings.

Another post-war user of the Albatros fighters was Czechoslovakia, which obtained several Austrian D.IIIs to equip its first Air Force units. And Canadian ace Raymond Collishaw, while flying for the White Russian forces during the Russian Civil War in 1919, reported shooting down an Albatros D.V carrying Red Russian markings.